NO ONE DOES IT LIKE YOU

& 77 OTHER ILLUSTRATED AFFIRMATIONS

AMY ROSE SPIEGEL

Illustrations by
CATHERINE WILLEMSE

Workman Publishing ✳ **New York**

For Heidi, Lito, and Hermione Hoby

Text copyright © 2019 by Amy Rose Spiegel
Illustrations copyright © 2019 by Catherine Willemse

Library of Congress Cataloging-in-Publication Data is available.

ISBN: 978-1-5235-0531-9

Design by Rae Ann Spitzenberger
Author photo by Jordan Hemingway

Backgrounds from shutterstock.com

Workman books are available at special discounts when purchased in bulk for premiums and sales promotions as well as for fund-raising or educational use. Special editions or book excerpts can also be created to specification. For details, contact the Special Sales Director at the address below, or send an email to specialmarkets@workman.com.

Workman Publishing Co., Inc.
225 Varick Street
New York, NY 10014-4381
workman.com

WORKMAN is a registered trademark of Workman Publishing Co., Inc.

Printed in China
First printing February 2019

10 9 8 7 6 5 4 3 2 1

Introduction

One bad summer, I was passing an afternoon by languishing in my sadness in the backyard garden of a crumbling apartment two friends and I chose, poorly, to move into together. (We somehow overlooked the syringe-filled kiddie pool in an alleyway beneath my window.) Bearing down on me was this thought: *So much was wrong*—things with a boyfriend hadn't worked out, I was broke and disrespected at work, and many-tentacled family dramas refused to loosen their grip. Plus, I loathed my hair, face, and personality!

That day, I got a call from someone I love. Too low to pretend brightness, I moaned for 17 minutes. She listened, then said, "Can you change how you sit in a chair? Can you make how you exist in the immediate world around you slightly different?" Among other pieces of advice, she told me to get it together: "Look, you need to go be the fucking moon." My voice sounded different when we hung up.

I very likely don't know you. Still, if you're *going through it*, I hope I can offer you some of the ease that call instilled in me. I am no longer acquainted with the kiddie pool; my debt has lessened; I found a new job that I love. (I continue to work on perfecting my posture and becoming the moon, but I'm certain I'm closer than ever.) The sentences in this book were the bridges I used to arrive in a slightly different immediate world, and I still use them often. Sometimes holding one thought close makes the rest legible.

You are the
only authority
on yourself.

Some things are good
even when they're bad:
infomercials, junk food,
roadside attractions,
homemade gifts, Ferris
wheels, romance novels,
and parts of you, too.

The advice you need
most can almost always
come from yourself.

Gild the kingdom
of your brain:
Keep researching.

Your life is a brand-new invention—construct it however you want.

Imitate whom you imagine is the greatest version of yourself.

Concentration doesn't
come automatically. Decide
where you want to apply your
focus, then act that way.

There's rarely a solid
reason to pretend like
you don't know right from
wrong, no matter what
you're surrounded by that
seems to contradict that.

Weaponized productivity—
hard work that feels
self-sacrificial or painfully
excludes the rest of your
life—is likely a waste
of your time.

Picture yourself as a little kid. Remember the promises you want to keep to that person.

This moment is only
one part of your day,
week, year, life.

Give people a reason to remember your conversations, whether you do that by speaking or listening.

Your only permanent
homes are your body and
your memories, and you
take both everywhere.

You are allowed to
be unruly. It doesn't
make you a mess.

Doing something only
you know about—whatever it
is—can make you feel like you
have one over on the world,
which is occasionally the
best feeling around.

If you don't like who
you are around a person,
go be someone else
with someone else.

Keep good secrets
for yourself.

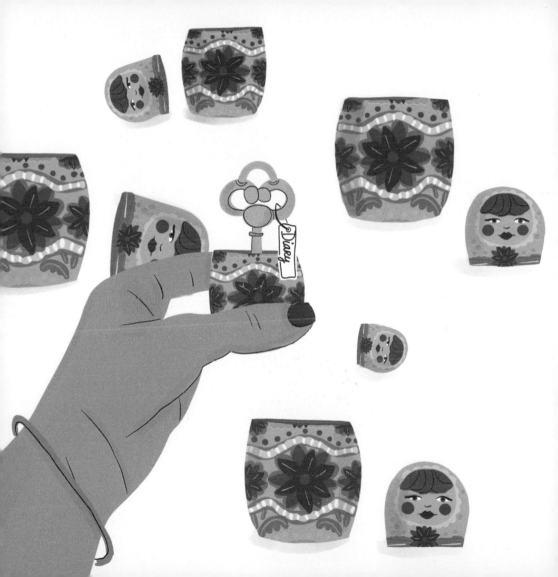

Intimacy isn't
inborn—it's carefully,
reciprocally earned.

Some habits feel great until they, for whatever reason, don't anymore. Do what you actually *like* to do, not just what you're accustomed to doing.

There are countless things you've never done before, including taking this next breath.

Frankness, communicated thoughtfully, can be one of the highest forms of respect.

Your work isn't frivolous.
Your heart isn't frivolous.

You know what you believe. You can double-check your trust of it by questioning it and by allowing your thoughts to be mutable. (This is commonly referred to as "maturity.")

Notice others' innocence
before you decide their guilt.

Your ethics and politics
are your architecture;
build up those convictions
and you'll have built a life.

It's so exciting and rad to fall in love, even if you're the only person who ever knows you did. Try to do it often.

You can't allow the fear of no one ever *getting it* to impede the goodness and closeness that can come from presenting the truth of your heart.

Grow something worth
championing, defending,
and giving to the world.

Demanding perfection
from yourself and others
is fruitless and unkind.
Less than ideal is way better.

You know so few of the people alive right now; feel lucky that you've found the ones you love, and eagerly anticipate the rest.

There are many different kinds of water. Ice cubes, rain, the shower, tears, seltzer. You are about half water, too.

**Someone thinks
you're funny on purpose,
even when you didn't
mean to be.**

The more unusual you can
make your day, the more
you stand to be awed by it.

Carve out your own world.

———————o———————

For a momentary
respite, look at or listen
to something smart,
beautiful, or hysterical,
and wholly unrelatable
to the scene at hand.

**Imagine how powerful
you'd be if you saw
what others do in you.**

You *are*, in fact, just the "kind of person" to do whatever you're doubting; by definition, nothing you do is too "unlike" you.

It can be fun and galvanizing
to have a nemesis, especially
if you're kind to them.

Being honest about what
you hope for and are
working toward isn't a jinx.

When you're into a person,
pay loving attention to them
as though you intend
to write their biography.

Regard yourself
as the moon;
wash everything
in your light.

When you're inclined
to introduce a thought with
"I'm sorry, but . . ." make sure
what you're saying is worth
the sincerity and weight
that an apology deserves.

Someone out there
reads your horoscope
just after they read their
own, or even before.

Friendship is an optional relationship—give and receive good reasons for maintaining each of yours.

Speak slowly, loudly, and clearly whenever possible; you'll believe yourself more readily.

When you're looking back
at what your life has been,
realize, with kindness,
that you did what you had
to do. Let that help you
understand how you're
trying to do even better.

Tell the truth—decorate
your entire life with it.

**When you're tempted to say
"I don't know," consider that
you *do*, and try that instead.**

Familial love and discord can be equally instructive in exemplifying the kind of love you want to give and be given.

**Every time you wake up,
you choose the world.**

Certain people might
not understand what
you're making right now,
but you have to keep at
it, and later, some will.

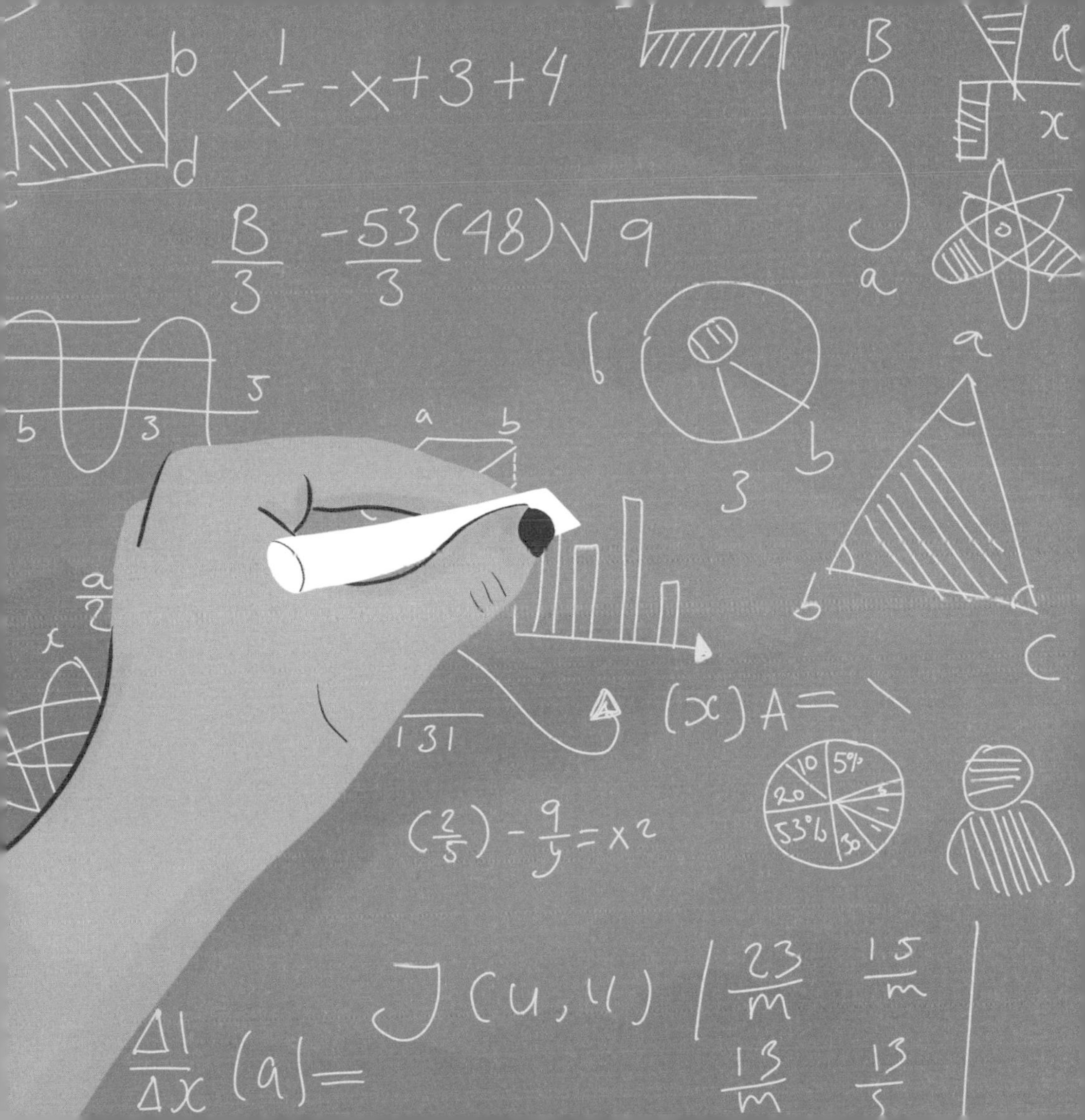

Are you defining something (or someone) by what it isn't, instead of what it is? If so, ask why.

Most of how life advances comes from simply putting on a clean shirt, leaving the house, and making eye contact once you arrive wherever you're going.

You can be evidence of goodness for others.

———— o ————

Convince yourself "I might as well" in order to dismantle the potency of whatever task is intimidating you, and then the next and next.

Pick your own favorite aspects of the world. You're not obliged to comply with anyone else's idea of what joy is supposed to be.

Everyone has their own methodology—you don't need to see alternative choices as corrections to your own.

You can treat any place
on earth, no matter your
familiarity with it, as your
home or as the place you're
taking a vacation; you'll
be right either way.

o———o

Money isn't dignity, or even that dignified, and it's definitely not an antidepressant.

Anyone, of any vocation or temperament, can enjoy the pleasures of a sick alter ego.

Even when you love it,
work can sometimes be the
worst—remember that wild
things can happen when
you just *finish the thing*.

Decide what kind of
impression you'd like
to have on others' moods
and lives, because you leave
one in every encounter.

No one does it like you.

You can usually stop freaking
out for long enough to write
a note to a person you like
about how they're doing.

You're the product of many lives before you—so much happened in order for you to be here. You encompass more people than one; in that way, you're never alone.

Solitude can work in
your favor if you use it
to hone the next iteration
of your greatness.

You're always going to be in your own company, so it's better to be your own best friend than an agitator or adversary.

What might happen if you tried to recognize what's right—both what's happening to you, and what you yourself are doing—instead of what's wrong?

How lucky to find and wrestle with something that feels difficult, rather than dull.

Your family, god bless them, doesn't get to decide who you arc.

You have the right to fail.
It can be a pleasure.

In the future, you will absolutely look back at photos of yourself and wish that you had understood how good you looked in that moment. Expedite that process.

There's no need to "have it all" to have more than enough.

Whenever you feel like nothing matters, realize that, by definition, that also means you can do whatever the hell you want. (When you do, everything will unquestionably matter much more.)

**Fucking up is
how you go pro.**

Revision is always
an option.

Even when you're already grateful: You have more than you know, and even more coming.

Don't suffer fools;
crack yourself up;
keep trying.

Acknowledgments

Thank you to Dan Kirschen, Laia Garcia, John McElwee, Thora Siemsen, Julianne Escobedo Shepherd, Bayukh Sen, Sarah Nicole Prickett, Kyle Wagner, Essie Lil, Dimitri Stathas, Brenda Cullerton, Laura and Madeline Spiegel, Jia Tolentino, Meredith Graves, Mitch Swenson, Jasmine Sanders, the GPG, Loren Olsen, lasagna, and the Mrat. To Catherine Willemse, Rachael Mt. Pleasant, Rae Ann Spitzenberger, and everyone at Workman. To my family, friends, and the other kinds of people I love.

About the Author

Amy Rose Spiegel is a writer and editor living in New York City. She is the author of *Action: A Book About Sex* (Grand Central), and her work has appeared in the *New York Times*, *Rolling Stone*, the *Guardian*, the *FADER*, and many other publications. She is a senior editor at Broadly, VICE's channel about identity, and previously edited at Rookie and BuzzFeed.